MW01615308

Surviving
A Disaster

**Evacuation Strategies And
Emergency Kits For Staying Alive**

Tony Nester

For Billy
Thanks for your friendship and for
Always being there on the trail.
You're a good man!
Peace amigo.
Tony

Diamond Creek Press, Flagstaff, Arizona

SURVIVING A DISASTER
Evacuation Strategies and Emergency Kits for Staying Alive

Copyright October 2007 by Tony Nester

Published by Diamond Creek Press
PO Box 2068
Flagstaff, AZ 86003
1-928-526-2552
www.apathways.com
Email: info@apathways.com

ISBN 0-9713811-2-7
Library of Congress Control Number:

Printed in the United States of America.

Dealer inquiries to the above address

Photos provided by Jim Cole, except for photos on pages 5, 7, 55 and 56. Copyright October 2007, www.jimcolephoto.com.

Disclaimer
    The information provided in this book is for academic purposes only. The author made every effort to ensure the information was correct at the time of publication and the author and Diamond Creek Press assume no liability for any laws broken by the reader nor any personal injury or injury to any-one else for the use or misuse of the information contained in this book.
    Visit us at www.apathways.com for information on our other books or survival training courses.

Acknowledgments

Putting together a book involves far more than the work of the writer and I would like to thank the many fine contributors who helped to shape this project. They include: Doug Ritter, Ian McDevitt, Doug Little, Randy Miller, Billy Meyer, and Elliot Spaulding. I also want to acknowledge fellow survival instructors Mike Masek and Gary Fox both of whom provided invaluable editing and input. Special thanks to photographer extraordinaire Jim Cole for shooting the photos. A heartfelt thanks to the many real-life survivors and first responders who willingly shared their harrowing experiences during the unfolding of this manuscript and kept my thinking grounded in reality. I am also grateful to the fine staff at the Center For Disease Control in Phoenix, Arizona who fielded many questions on post-disaster issues.

Finally, I want to thank my wife and children who continually remind me how precious life is and the duty we have to protect it.

Also by Tony Nester

Practical Survival Tips, Tricks, & Skills

Desert Survival Tips, Tricks, & Skills

Finding Food In The Wilds: Practical Hunting & Gathering Methods
(forthcoming)

Contents

INTRODUCTION

If you are reading this book, then you may be growing ever more concerned about the delicate fabric that holds our communities and world together. With more people on the planet today and with a complex, interdependent network of services providing for our daily needs, there is a greater call for each of us to be more self-reliant and take the helm of preparing our family for a disaster.

Whether you live in an area prone to earthquakes or hurricanes or you are worried about the potential for acts of terrorism, the information in this book can be of benefit by providing a place to start being prepared.

Where I live in the parched Southwestern US, wildfires pose a serious hazard each summer. As a result of living with this threat, my family has experienced the importance of having bail-out gear and emergency plans already in place if a blaze gets too close to our community. The whole process of loading the van with our emergency kits, grabbing the kids and dogs, and hitting the road is something we have down to 15 minutes and we've had to pull out on more than one occasion. While it is stressful to evacuate, the preparations we have made allow us to do so quickly and efficiently.

Formulating escape plans and assembling disaster supplies for your family can seem like daunting tasks until you learn to separate your wants from your actual needs. The former is a luxury, the latter is what can make all the difference in whether you live at all.

Like my other books on survival, this one is designed to cut to the chase and provide practical, field-tested information that the average person can use. The material contained herein comes from extensive personal experience and from interviews with actual survivors who have weathered out disasters around the country. It is not another rehashed checklist of emergency items written from the comfort of a couch. If it appears here, it is because it has worked under real-world conditions.

Most books about surviving disasters assume that the individual is going to be holed up at home for an extended period of time and living off of a considerable amount of stockpiled food and resources. Many fine books have been written on preparing your home, handling food storage,

1

& other issues pertinent to staying put. FEMA, Red Cross, and Homeland Security all have their recommended home survival kits, but what happens if you have to evacuate your home within minutes? Or if you are away on business, or on the other side of the city, when disaster strikes? How do you form an escape plan to cope with such a disaster? What essentials should you have on hand for quickly evacuating? What are the necessary skills for coping with life during an event where returning home is not an option? As the nation witnessed during the Hurricane Katrina debacle, first responders and relief workers can be overwhelmed for days or even weeks after a disaster. The sobering reality is that you are on your own.

This book addresses the above issues from the standpoint of someone needing to evacuate their home and be completely self-contained with only the provisions they can stow in their vehicle or on their back. In essence, survival on the run.

In the pages that follow, we'll look at suggestions for how to map out your particular region for possible escape routes, what emergency gear is essential, how to assemble a quality first-aid kit for your family, what's involved in procuring safe water, and the pertinent survival priorities for relocating to a safer area.

This book is also about fostering a preparedness mindset. My philosophy is that the more you know and the more skills you possess, the more options you have in life. So welcome to the empowering world of self-reliance, not only is it a necessity in today's world- it is your birthright as a member of the human race.

THE REALITY OF DISASTERS

In a large-scale disaster, there are certain realities that will reveal themselves rather quickly. Some of the common threads that run through both natural and human-caused disasters are:

1. First Responders and rescue workers will be overwhelmed. They may not physically be able to get to your location for days or even weeks depending on your area and the nature of the disaster.

2. The power grid could be down for long periods of time thus rendering water, gas, sanitation and other home utilities unusable. Fresh drinking water in particular will be at a premium.

3. Others in your community (including family & friends) will be totally unprepared and looking to you for help.

4. In extreme cases, it's going to be every one out for themselves as otherwise law-abiding citizens scramble to snatch up finite resources (food, water, meds) at any expense in order to stay alive.

5. There will be opportunistic thugs present to exploit the weak. Urban predators and possibly even gangs will be on the prowl.

6. There will be shortages of fuel for driving so you may be on foot once your vehicle hits empty.

7. And then there's Murphy's Law which is always present in our lives: a snow storm could also roll in, you sustain an injury, maybe you are battling the flu when the disaster hits, or it's the middle of the night when the city goes silent.

There are no guarantees in life. Being PREPARED AND PLANNING AHEAD are the keys to your longevity.

A Rumble To Remember

The North Ridge earthquake that struck California in 1994 killed 57 people and seriously injured 1,500 more. After the quake, 9,000 businesses and homes were without electricity and more than 48,000 were without water. For days afterward, another 22,000 people were homeless due to the severe damage to entire neighborhoods.

WHAT IT TAKES TO PREVAIL

Your priorities when Life is driven into a corner during a disaster are:

- Having the Proper Mindset
- Tending to Injuries
- Protecting Yourself
- Staying Hydrated
- Staying Warm & Dry
- Taking Care of Hygiene
- Getting Rest

Having The Proper Mindset

When confronted with a catastrophe, there are two attitudes to choose from: 1) The role of a Helpless Victim 2) The role of an Optimistic Survivor. The mindset you choose will determine how well you make it through the disaster at hand.

We humans have survival hardwired into our genes but our modern, cushy lifestyles have made that reality fade into the background. Once the veneer of civilization gets peeled away, as in a disaster, your true character will be revealed.

Sometimes, under the extreme conditions that survivors face, life can get rough, so if the lights go out and the odds are pitted against you, dig deep inside yourself and declare: "I am not going out without a fight. I will be here tomorrow and the next day!" Without the will to live, little else in this book matters. What will it be: Victim or Survivor? Decide now.

Tending To Injuries

Many disasters have injury and trauma associated with the event. Collapsed buildings, debris from floodwater, toxic spills, and structural fires are just a few of the hazards that befall urban survivors. Having a quality first-aid kit and knowing the basics of how to control bleeding, stabilize injuries, and perform CPR are essential life skills that every human being should know regardless of a disaster. You may have to self-rescue and tend to your own wounds or assist someone in your family.

4

A stocked vehicle ready to roll.

I highly recommend to all my students that they take at least a 2-day Wilderness First-Aid class which covers a variety of ways for handling injuries under challenging conditions. Your local Red-Cross and fire departments also offers hands-on courses in First-Aid & CPR.

Protecting Yourself

In large-scale disasters, lawlessness will quickly follow any major break-down in infrastructure and you need to have the means of protecting your-self from the urban predators who will be out in force as chaos sweeps over the community.

First responders and police officers will be overwhelmed and may not be able to provide city-wide protection against the opportunistic thugs who are going to be roaming the area. During Katrina, New Orleans looked more like a war zone than a U.S. city where heavily armed gangs roamed the streets in the days after the storm hit.

You may be thinking- "Well, the (choose one: mayor, national guard, police, government)_____ won't let that happen." I truly hope they don't but I wouldn't stake my family's safety on it. In a large-scale disaster chances are good that No One will come to your aid. Again, you alone are responsible for safeguarding your loved ones. For many people, a firearm comes to mind as the answer to self-protection. However, this entails more than going to the local gun shop and buying a .45 and some ammo. I don't recommend having a gun unless you have first received training from a competent instructor. Otherwise, you will be a danger to, not only yourself, but others around you, including your family. If you choose a firearm for home defense then invest in the time and training it takes to become proficient.

If you are planning for the areas of food, water, and medical then you also have to consider how you are going to defend your family. At the very least, consider carrying a legal weapon like pepper spray or receiving training in a practical self-defense style like Krav Maga or Jiu-Jitsu.

Staying Hydrated

Obtaining clean drinking water and staying hydrated are critical to survival in any environment. One of the major post-disaster concerns is going to be avoiding dysentery and hepatitis from contaminated water sources found in an urban setting. Worldwide, 6000 people die each day of waterborne diseases, mostly in third world countries, but third world survival conditions are what you may be confronted with following a large scale disaster in your region.

Following the 1994 North Ridge earthquake in California, the resulting infrastructure damage left thousands of people without fresh water. Other sources were either non-existent or contaminated with a soup of toxins. Health agencies informed the public to use supplies like bottled water but with extensive damage to the roads it was nearly impossible to provide stranded survivors with fresh drinking water.

Food supplies will also be quickly depleted due to transportation networks being damaged along with food spoilage due to a loss of refrigeration. Food you can live without and we will discuss this in greater depth in the pages ahead. Water you must have or you could succumb to dehydration. Whether you are an Olympic athlete or a Green Beret, you can't go without it. Fresh drinking water will be at a premium in a disaster.

In the pages that follow you will learn reliable means of procuring and purifying tainted water in an emergency. The best indicator for checking if you are hydrated is if you are peeing clear fluid. If not, then drink up! For parents coping with a disaster, you have to make sure young children are drinking plenty of fluids and to remember that kids are not little adults. They have their own physiological needs that differ from grownups.

Being able to procure fresh water, in both urban and wilderness settings, is essential for surviving the aftermath of a disaster. Having at least two gallons per person per day in your home emergency kit will save you from tapping into questionable water sources.

The Fire That Couldn't Be Quenched

The Rodeo-Chediski Fire was the worst wildfire in the history of Arizona. It began in June of 2002 and swept across the pine forests of central Arizona consuming over 467,000 acres and over 350 homes.

I remember seeing the giant orange mushroom cloud at night from my home well over 100 miles away. Entire communities and up to 30,000 people were evacuated from their homes as the fire blazed out of control for nearly three weeks.

Many people who were unprepared lost everything they owned and literally escaped with only the clothes on their backs. Having emergency gear stowed at home and the ability to evacuate within 15 minutes is essential if you live in a region prone to wildfires.

Staying Warm & Dry

Hypothermia is the number one killer of people in the outdoors the world over. If you are in a disaster survival situation in the colder months be aware that the elements are another factor to consider when preparing your emergency kits. Especially when it comes to clothing selection. Clothing is the first shelter system you have so make sure it consists of quality garments (i.e., not cotton). This means clothes made from wool, fleece, or silk. I prefer a layering system: 5 upper body garments consisting of a Coolmax t-shirt, turtleneck, flannel shirt, wool sweater, and insulated coat with a hood. In addition, a pair of long-underwear, an extra pair of wool socks, and good boots complete the wardrobe. Lastly, I always have a sleeping bag stowed in my vehicle. Nowadays these compress down to the size of a loaf of bread and can keep you warm in the bitter cold.

Taking Care of Hygiene

Hygiene is of tremendous importance in preventing the spread of many types of infections like hepatitis, dysentery, and stomach ailments that are often transmitted by dirty hands or contaminated food or water. Given the enormity of our urban populations, hygiene will certainly be an issue in the aftermath of an urban disaster.

Frequent washing of your hands or using hand sanitizer will serve as a preventative measure. Keep a small bottle of hand-sanitizer in the glove box of each vehicle. Strive to wash your hands several times a day, especially before eating or handling food. Wearing shoes or boots, as opposed to sandals, will also help protect your feet and prevent infection from contaminated water sources or debris.

In urban areas where the waterlines are damaged, many toilets will still flush if fresh water is added to the bowl. If you are on the road and have to use nature's restroom, then dig a hole 4"-6" deep in the dirt and bury any waste.

Getting Rest

Getting sleep or just catnapping becomes paramount the longer your ordeal lasts. The reader has no doubt been sleep deprived before for a few days but, in a disaster, you may also be facing injuries, food and water deprivation, extreme weather, and the stress of taking care of your family.

As noted in my previous books on survival, sleep is a priority in both urban and wilderness emergencies. The amount you get will affect your health, mindset, & physical abilities. Take it when it comes, even if only in increments.

What Are The Disasters Of Concern For Your Region?

Natural Disasters

Earthquake
Epidemic/Bird Flu
Floods
Dam collapse
Volcanic eruption
Snowstorm
Tropical storm
Tornado
Landslide
Power shortage
Tsunami and tidal wave

Human Caused Disasters

Terrorist attack
Industrial/technological accident
Chemical spills
Nuclear explosion
Oil spill
Structural fires
Forest/grassland fire

Keep in mind that disasters rarely respect geographic boundaries on the map.

SURVIVAL ON THE RUN: ESCAPING A DISASTER

The four places you might be confronted with a survival situation during a disaster:

- At Home
- At Work
- In Your Vehicle
- Traveling (away on business)

Understanding the specific threats unique to your region will help you identify the potential escape routes and survival issues associated with evacuating from any of the above four locations and what your response would be to both short-range and long-range disasters. Residing in a sparsely populated region presents different evacuation issues than living in a large metropolis.

There are three geographic areas to consider when formulating your escape plan: Local, Regional, and Statewide. Local refers to your immediate neighborhood or suburb. Regional is the entire city where your neighborhood is contained. Statewide embodies all of the cities within the state where you reside.

Lay out a map of your state, get three sheets of paper, and answer the questions for the scenarios on the following pages. By mentally rehearsing now, when the waters are calm, you will dramatically increase your family's odds of having a smooth voyage should you have to evacuate before a disaster.

Local Disaster: Evacuating Beyond Your Neighborhood

If there were an approaching wildfire or a chemical spill near your home, what is the fastest way to gain 15 miles of distance from the threat? This is a short-term emergency where you will be evacuating for 24-48 hours.

Things to consider:

- Map out the advantages and disadvantages of heading in any of the four directions from your house.

• What are the capabilities of the hospital in your region and what level of trauma can they handle?

• What are the areas with the heaviest crime along these four directions and how can you circumvent traveling near them?

• What friends or family do you have along the four directions that you could call on for assistance?

• Where will you stay if you can't return home for two or three days?

• How will these above considerations change during the winter months vs. the summer months for your specific area?

With much of the western U.S. a tinderbox, you need to have an escape plan in place if your home borders the forest.

Regional Disaster: Evacuating Beyond Your City

Next, look at how your plan would change if the threat were regional. For example, what would be your best escape route(s) during a disaster where the entire city is affected by a catastrophe, such as a hurricane or an earthquake.

Instead of having to clear a 15-mile radius from your house as in the previous example, here you might have to gain at least 60 miles and not be able to return home for a week or more.

Things to consider:

• Get out while the going is good. If you know the storm or threat is coming, don't waste precious minutes as thousands of others, who delay, will be clogging the roads.

• What would your plan be if you couldn't reach your children at school? Is there someone who can pick them up in your absence and where is the predetermined meeting spot for you to all reconnect?

• Again, map out the four directions of travel from your city and the best routes to take. These may be secondary highways or roads rather than the large interstates that are burdened under normal conditions.

• What is waiting for you on the other end? Are you going to drive to another city, into the country, or still be traveling on a remote stretch of highway after 60 miles?

• What medical facilities are available enroute and what are their trauma capabilities?

• Any areas of concern regarding high-crime neighborhoods along these routes?

• Any friends or family to stay with along the way?

• Again, how will this look in the winter vs. the summer?

• If for some reason, your vehicle broke down or the roads were impassable and you had to walk, how would this escape plan change?

Seeking Shelter

Emergency shelters established by the city or government in a large scale catastrophe might be considered a place of temporary refuge but keep in mind that once you check in you may not be able to leave until the authorities grant permission. In some cases, items such as food, water, medical supplies, and firearms will be confiscated for the greater good and you will essentially be relegated to the role of dependent. You may wish to register your name with shelter staff outside to help other family members locate you but carefully consider your options before entering and relinquishing your freedom.

Statewide Disaster: Evacuating Beyond State Lines

You are eating dinner at home when you catch the news about a nuclear reactor melting down south of the city. The winds could be carrying contaminated air your way within a short time. Heading north, upwind of the reactor, is out of the question so you have to drive east or west to avoid exposure.

Can you be ready to pull out in 15 minutes?

Things to consider:

Let's assume that this epic catastrophe will prevent you from ever returning to your home, so in addition to your regular emergency gear, what else would you take, room permitting?

• Thousands of other "refugees" will be arriving in the outlying cities you will be driving to. How long will your own provisions last since stores will be quickly depleted?

• How far can your vehicle travel on one tank of gas?

If the roads were impassable, how would this change your direction of travel if you were on foot?

• What resources lay ahead at your destination? Will you stay with friends, camp out in the woods, or sleep in your vehicle?

• Again, what are the medical facilities and trauma capabilities like in the outlying cities?

• Where are the crime-ridden areas along the way?

• What are these routes like in the winter vs. the summer months?

• What is your plan for getting food and water after your short-term supply runs out?

* * *

As you can see from answering these questions, each of these evacuation scenarios has unique concerns. Every disaster provides us with lessons in how to be prepared. Study them in the newspaper and ask yourself: "What if it happened here?" You will respond during a crisis according to how you have mentally rehearsed and physically prepared.

This section was about exercising that survival tool between your ears. The next section will delve into the emergency gear for coping with life during and after an evacuation from your home.

ASSEMBLING QUALITY EMERGENCY KITS

The main theme underlying self-reliance is the mental attitude of being prepared and planning ahead. You don't want to be in the kind of situation where you just evacuated your house and are caught with only the clothes on your back and now have to locate food, water, and medical supplies for your family.

You need to have the escape routes picked out ahead of time and be ready to roll with all of your gear and family members within 15 minutes of the decision to evacuate. Take the time NOW to assemble a few emergency kits that will sustain you during a crisis.

This section breaks down the contents of three types of affordable, emergency kits as well as discussing how to put together a quality medical kit. While your kits might look different than mine in terms of the types of gear it contains, it should be able to take care of the physical priorities mentioned earlier. You are striving to provide for First Aid, Personal Defense, Water, Staying Warm & Dry, and Hygiene.

Look over this section, make a list of the items you need for your lifestyle and location, and then begin to assemble your gear. I have my own kits broken down to four key areas:

- Everyday Carry Items
- Shoulder Bag or Get-Back-Home Kit
- Home Bail Out Kit
- Survivors First-Aid Kit

When it comes to survival gear, the principle of layering is important to understand. With critical gear, you don't want all of your eggs in one basket so to speak. If you lose or have to ditch your Home Bail-Out Kit, then you have got the Shoulder Bag; if that fails then you still have your Every Day Carry items in your pockets. Essentially, a back up to a back up to a back up is what you are after here. With each step up in kit size you build on the previous kit's contents.

The Everyday Carry Items and Shoulder Bag are designed to carry the essential, bare-bones survival gear to get you through a short-term crisis. The Home Bail-Out Kit is more extensive and allows you to carry what you need to LIVE, not just survive, since you'll be stuffing this kit in your car where space is less of an issue.

EVERY DAY CARRY ITEMS

This is simply pocket gear. My Every Day Carry Items are built around a Cold Steel folding knife with a 3" blade, BIC lighter, a key chain micro-flashlight, cell-phone, cash, and wallet. Nothing major here, most people carry this stuff. Just make sure you have quality items.

Given my propensity for being hungry, I usually throw a Clif Bar in a pocket and, since I live in the desert Southwest, water is always carried with me even on a short drive.

The modern urban survival kit.

THE SHOULDER BAG OR GET-BACK-HOME KIT

This is a lightweight Shoulder Bag (courier's bag) or backpack stowed in your office or vehicle with enough basic gear to let you travel on foot, if need be. If it's lightweight you are more likely to carry it with you as opposed to a cumbersome hockey duffel bag. As noted during recent disasters, some evacuees had to walk forty miles or more out of their city before supplies were available! This is where the almighty Shoulder-Bag comes in to play. With this gear you are able to meet the needs of shelter, water, medical, and self-protection.

Low-profile and inconspicuous are key here- avoid the camouflaged, commando-style gear. You want to blend in and look like a student with a book bag and not like a Navy Seal. Also, avoid the orange packs with "Survival Gear" stamped on it unless you want those less prepared to know that you are stocked with supplies.

I have also seen fishing & camera vests turned into decent survival vests that blend in well and carry a full a compliment of gear. The idea here is to create a survival kit that will sustain you for 24-48 hours as you flee the disaster stricken area.

Two examples of quality shoulder bags for carrying basic survival gear.

My Shoulder Bag Contents

- LED Mini-Flashlight w/extra battery
- 32 oz Collapsible water container
- 1 16 oz Nalgene water bottle with a few passes of duct tape wrapped around
- 3 Firestarters: 2 Bic lighters & 1 box REI Stormproof Matches
- 6 Met-RX Meal-Replacement Bars
- 4 oz bag of Jerky
- 3 HydraLyte rehydration packets
- 1 Bottle Potable Aqua water purification tablets
- 2 dust masks
- Compass (or GPS)
- Local and state maps for my region
- Important phone contacts of family members
- Photos of my kids (hundreds of kids were lost and alone after Katrina)
- Spare (prescription) glasses
- Small 1st-aid kit
- Handheld AM/FM/Shortwave Radio
- 12 oz enamel cup
- Leatherman Wave
- Cash—small bills of $5, 10s, & 20s along with $10 in quarters & change
- Sunscreen
- 2 Bandannas
- 1 large trash bag
- 1 Army-style poncho
- 50' of 1/8" diameter rope
- Leather gloves
- Pepper spray or firearm

Ideally, the weight of the entire Shoulder Bag should not exceed 20 pounds.

Globetrotter's Survival Kit

If you are a business traveler and spend a considerable amount of time flying around the country or globe, then consider preparing a stripped down version of the Shoulder Bag in case you ever have to survive in a disaster-riddled city. Such a kit should be lightweight and contain: cash, passport, relevant maps, small first-aid kit, a few protein bars, flashlight, cellphone and charger, water purification tablets, and spare clothes. You may want to add an innocuous multi-tool like a Swiss-Tech 9-in-1 which lacks a blade but has many useful features. This gear can fit in a small fannypack but remember to check airline regulations as they are constantly changing.

HOME BAIL-OUT KIT: Your Family Gear

The Home Bail-Out Kit is made up of the contents of the Shoulder Bag and much more. Stowed in a closet and ready to go, your Home Bail-Out Kit goes beyond short-term survival items and is intended for a week or more of living on the road. Remember the goal here is to be able to evacuate your home within 15 minutes. This is not gear you rush around the house collecting when you hear the city's emergency sirens blaring. We have our family gear packed in several duffel bags along with two large Tupperware containers for the food.

How Much Gear & Food Should I Have?

You want as much as you can carry or stash in your vehicle so, if possible, go beyond the endlessly touted 72-hour preparation list pushed by federal agencies. Psychologically it will boost your morale and you may also have extra family members who arrive unprepared. Besides any extra chow or supplies can always be used for bartering.

Included on the list below are many luxury items and a greater range of food than was present with the Shoulder Bag.

Here is an example of our family kit for 4 people (and one big dog) for seven days:

My Home Bail-Out Kit Contents

- One-burner stove & 2 propane canisters
- MSR brand water filter
- 1 Bottle of Potable Aqua Iodine purification tablets
- 2-way radios
- 4 one quart water bottles, wrapped with a few passes of duct tape
- 2 seven gallon water jugs
- 100' of 1/8" diameter rope
- 2 Mora knives (fixed blade)
- 4 Sleeping bags
- 2 Army ponchos
- 2 rolls of toilet paper
- Food (see the following list)
- Comprehensive 1st Aid kit
- Satellite phone and contact numbers
- Handheld AM/FM/Shortwave Radio
- 64 oz stainless cooking pot
- 4-person tent & ground tarp
- 2 pair spare socks per person
- Wool hat per person
- Fleece sweater per person
- Turtleneck per person
- Long underwear top per person
- Long underwear bottom per person
- Warm jacket per person
- Leather work gloves per person
- Spare prescription glasses
- Toothbrushes & toothpaste
- 8-ounce bottle of handsoap
- 4 Bandannas
- 4 Dust masks
- 4 Brimmed hats

- Sunscreen
- Pediatric 1st-aid book and copy of the book "Where There Is No Doctor"
- Relevant documents: tax records, bank statements, birth certificate, etc…
- Topographic maps of area
- .22 rifle and ammo
- Gun cleaning kit
- Fishing pole & gear
- 2 lighters
- Feminine sanitary items
- Cash—small bills of $5, 10, & 20s along with $10 in quarters

Bear in mind that this kit is an example of the gear I carry and recommend. Where you live will affect how you prepare. The city dweller is not going to have much need for the aforementioned fishing tackle for example. People residing in the country will also have different evacuation procedures than those in urban areas.

Food, water, and gear for one person and Fido for seven days.

A Keen-Edged Survivor

Books and endless websites abound on the ultimate survival knife. I have my preferred blades but they work for me and may not feel great for you, so find what works in your hands and then never leave home without it (though check your state's knife laws). A knife is an essential survival tool and must be with you to be of any good. As the Finnish say: "a knife-less man is a life-less man."

A few words of advice: avoid the hollow-handled knives as these are pure junk; carry both a fixed blade that has the tang extending through the handle and a quality folding blade (lockblade) with a 2"-3" blade (check your local knife laws), and learn how to sharpen your blade. Multi-tools are not knives, they are multi-tools so supplement your Leatherman or Gerber with a good knife. Also, keep in mind that having one of any critical piece of gear is a weak system. It is best to carry two knives.

Quality knives: Left to right, Cold Steel Voyager lock blades and two versions of Swedish Mora knives.

The blades I use the most are shown in the accompanying photo. I carry a 3" Cold Steel Voyager lockblade for generic tasks and a fixed blade Swedish Mora as my primary cutting tool. I also have a Leatherman Wave which is one of the better multi-tools available.

Regarding knife safety, keep in mind the following rules of the blade:
- Never carve towards yourself
- Be aware of others around you
- Make sure the knife is sharp
- A knife should either be in your hands because you are using it or back in its sheath because you are not using it. Don't stick it in a stump or leave it on the ground.

Financial Survival: Critical Papers & Documents

These documents can be critical in re-establishing your life if you lose everything else in your home during a disaster. All too often people assemble excellent survival kits only to forget about the documents below during the rush associated with evacuating.

- Birth certificates
- Tax returns
- Marriage license
- Social Security card
- Children's immunization records
- Passport
- Bank statements & passwords
- Medical insurance
- Will
- Drug prescriptions
- Pet & vet records
- Insurance policies
- Pertinent computer CDs

Save what you can on a CD or USB drive and also have hard copies. You may even want to have a back up CD stored at a relative's house. Lastly, do not forget to include your laptop if it contains valuable data.

Copies of these documents can be stored in a small Tupperware container and located next to your Home Bail-Out Kit.

While it is not a survival priority, consider including family photo albums and any irreplaceable heirlooms if space permits.

Cash Is King

Following a major disaster, the local economy along with banks and ATM's may be crippled. Plan on having extra cash on hand. Most survivors of catastrophes throughout the U.S. that I interviewed said that many store owners routinely jacked up the price of common items like bottled water, milk, and bread in the hours following a disaster. An earthquake survivor told me that a shopkeeper in his neighborhood was selling batteries for $10 a piece to desperate customers in the hours following the quake!

Experienced urban survivors recommended having $100–$200 on hand and that these be in the form of small bills like $5, $10s, and $20s along with a few rolls of quarters.

Food For The Home Bail-Out Kit

Most people preparing a Home Kit make the mistake of setting aside food for the lean times that they usually would not eat on a regular basis. A friend once told me his idea of food preparation for a long-term emergency was having a fifty pound bag of dry beans in the attic! I asked him if he even liked beans and he said, "Heck no, but it was cheap and it's only for a crisis."

In a true disaster, you are already going to be physically stressed so add good-tasting chow to the menu and not something too far off from what you would normally consume. Good food is also calming and reassuring for children and when they are happy, life is indeed good.

When preparing a family menu, I would recommend that you keep in mind the following principles:

• Whatever foods you decide upon, strive for a minimum of 1800 calories per person per day. More is better but you may have limited space in your vehicle.

• Bring foods that do not require cooking or refrigeration like tuna, canned soup, pasta, or chili (just remember to pack a can-opener!).

• Bring foods that can be made into one-pot meals. My favorite is a can of chicken with ravioli and nuts.

• Peanut butter is always a mainstay and tastes good on almost everything, plus it's super-high in calories and fat.

• Sweets are a great morale booster, especially for kids, so throw in some candy bars or chocolate.

• Don't forget pet food. You'll need enough of their regular food to last for at least a week as well as factoring in their water needs.

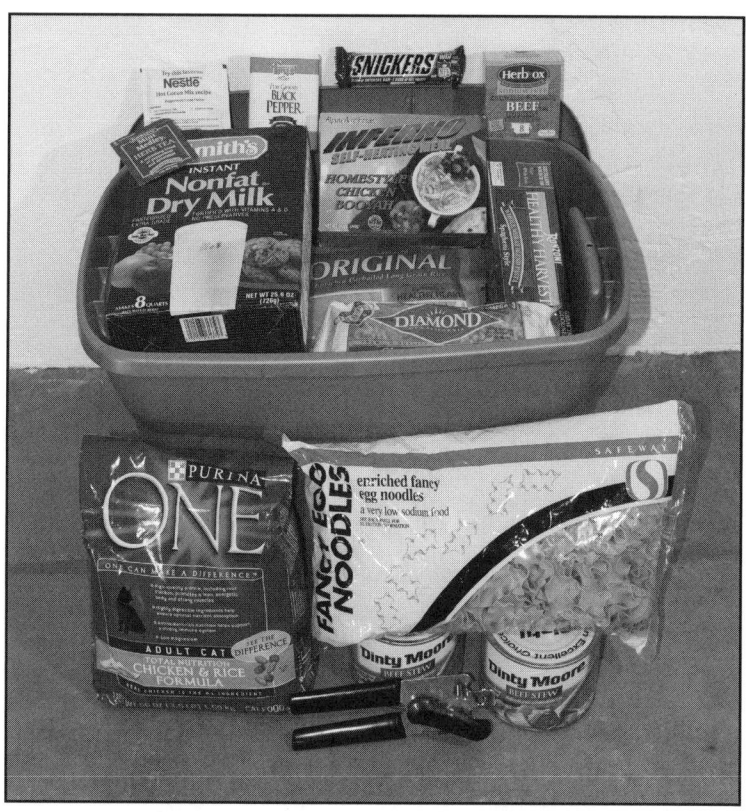

An assortment of dry and canned goods that make
simple one-pot meals along with pet food.

Our basic menu, for four people, consists of the following items designed to last 7 days on the road. It is essentially what we take for a weeklong car camping trip so we know it works for us:

- 3 lbs of white rice
- 6 cans of pinto beans
- 1 bottle of bouillon cubes (for sodium replacement)
- 3 lbs of dry pasta
- 2, 16 oz cans of spaghetti sauce
- 6 cans of chicken
- 12 packets of tuna
- 3 packets of quality jerky
- 2 cans of ravioli
- 2 boxes macaroni and cheese
- 64 oz can of nuts
- 2 cartons of soy milk
- 1 container of old-fashioned oatmeal
- 1 box of Crème-of-Wheat
- 1 box of granola-type cereal
- 1 lb of brown sugar
- 1 bag of raisins
- 2 lbs of assorted dried fruit like apricots, banana chips, etc…
- 1 large jar of peanut butter
- 1 large jar of jelly
- 2 dozen packets of tea and cocoa
- Spice Kit (see the info that follows)
- 2 boxes of wheat crackers
- 1 case of 24 assorted small juice boxes
- 5 lb bag of M & M's
- 2 packages of chocolate chip cookies
- 10 lb bag of dog food for 1 pooch
- Water: 2 gallons per person per day

Breakfasts consist of alternating days of oatmeal or Crème-of-wheat with dried fruit and granola mixed in. Lunches are usually salmon or tuna with crackers, canned ravioli, or jerky and dried fruit. Peanut butter and jelly are hard to beat as is mac-n-cheese. For dinners, we alternate with days of pasta with chicken or rice and beans.

Pass The Ketchup

Don't overlook the power of a spice kit! Having a few containers of spices and condiments can make any meal into a winner. Salt, black pepper, ginger, Tabasco sauce, brown sugar, bouillon cubes, & vinaigrette dressing are my favorites. Find what you like and toss some in with your food items. You won't regret it.

Meals are cooked on a propane stove. Notice also that we have a lot of dry foods that can be eaten cold in case cooking is not possible.

Eating well on the road or in the backcountry is a seemingly forgotten art but it really comes down to finding a couple of base dishes like rice or pasta that you can revolve everything else around.

Inspect and rotate food in your home-kit every six months and again pack only items you would normally eat.

What About Fido and Whiskers?

Do not plan on turning your animals loose after a disaster to scavenge for themselves. Include your cat/dog/horses in your escape plan. We have a forty pound bag of dog food included with our Home-Kit which will feed our pooch for one month. Also bring a collar with tags, a leash, and extra water. Keep in mind that pets are not allowed at most emergency shelters so you will need to find a pet-friendly motel.

SURVIVORS FIRST-AID KIT

Chances are good that trauma and debilitating injury will be present around you in a major disaster. This section is not intended to cover Gutter Medicine or how to perform a heart transplant on a subway but rather to direct you towards the resources that are out there for the average person to learn improvised medical skills. A hundred years ago, everyone possessed such skills but nowadays it's the Virtual Doctor online who provides the answers.

There are many outstanding workshops available (see Appendix) and I highly recommend augmenting your survival skills with at least a 2-day Wilderness First-Aid Course. You will learn how to stabilize injuries and improvise with what is at hand and these are mighty good things to know for both urban and wilderness settings. If you are a parent, you will be grateful to have such training even if you rarely venture into the wilds!

If nothing else, buy a copy of the book *Where There Is No Doctor* and study the chapters on hypothermia, heat-stress, and waterborne illness as these are the more common ailments you may have to face.

Finally, purchase one of the better First-Aid kits from either Atwater Carey or Adventure Medical Kits. This will be your first line of defense for handling illness and injury. These kits are far superior to the generic medical kits stuffed with colorful band-aids found at the pharmacy.

To further refine my kit, I've added the following items:

- ACE Wrap—hard to find stretchy fabric when you need it.
- PriMed Gauze—simply the best gauze material on the market for dealing with intense bleeding.
- Triangular bandage—myriad uses for tourniquets, slings, headwraps, straining water.
- Benadryl—critical for bug bites & anaphylactic shock. Get the Fast-Melt kids version.
- Steri Strips—for closing wounds until you can get stitched up by a doctor.
- Irrigation syringe—a must have item for first-aid kits. Great for blasting the nasty germs out of wounds.
- Immodium—for diarrhea.

• Tweezers—get a quality pair with thin, flat-nosed tips for removing splinters.
• Duct tape—for instant band-aids, covering blisters, fixing gear, and a hundred other uses.
• Hand-Sanitizer—or something similar to aid with hygiene.
• Personal Prescription Medications—a 2-week supply of extras as your pharmacy may be shut down.

Will this make you into a MASH doctor? Absolutely not but it will equip you to better handle the injuries that are often associated with a disaster and stack the odds in your favor until you can get to a hospital.

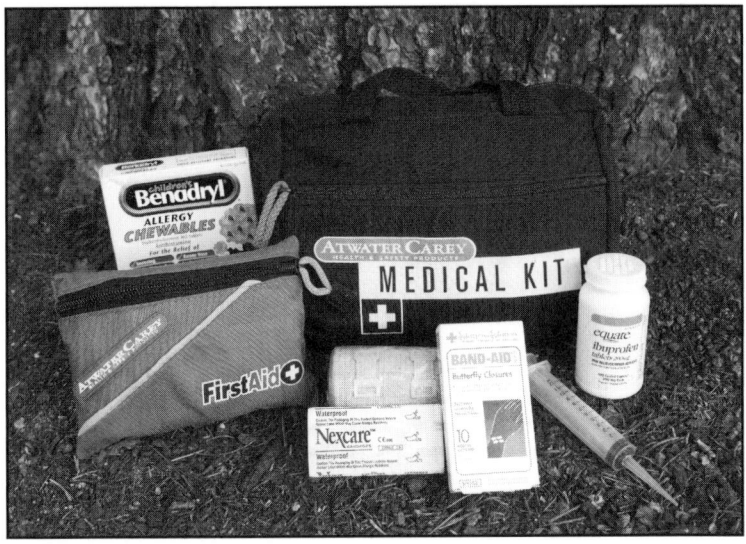

A small personal first aid kit on the left and a large family sized kit on the right, along with supplemental items to help cope with injury.

PREPARING CHILDREN FOR A CRISIS

A significant disruption of day-to-day life can take place in areas affected by a natural or human-caused disaster. Kids thrive on structure and when that is taken away by the resulting chaos of a crisis, stress and fear can take over. I've seen it in my own young children when we've had to prepare for an evacuation during encroaching wildfires. Even if my wife and I try to outwardly remain calm, our kids still pick up on our stress.

We now have a regular drill that we perform a few times a year. We talk about what to do if a wildfire gets too close, have the kids' "jobs" during the crisis defined, and discuss the Home Kit's location and uses.

For older kids, I'd recommend assigning them a task so they feel empowered and have a role to play. It can be something as simple as gathering up the family pets or loading the van during the evacuation. Kids need structure and a way to feel like they are in control. Assign them a role other than nervous bystander.

As a parent you will no doubt be trying to gather as much information as possible from media coverage of the disaster but try to reduce your kid's exposure to the events on TV. Images of catastrophe will only add to their anxiety levels. Keep in mind that with acute stress in children, you may see noticeable changes in their sleep patterns and behavior in the days and weeks following a disaster.

Children are not little adults. They handle turmoil and physical stress differently than a grownup so be even more vigilant with their needs.

You will also want to discuss with your children, who will pick them up from school if there is an emergency and you cannot be there. You will want to have this worked out with other family members or friends in advance.

You will find excellent information for preparing children on the American Academy of Pediatric's website at www.aap.org.

Shoulder Bag For The Kids

Each of my kids has a small Shoulder Bag which they have taken part in compiling. This gives them a sense of security knowing they have some goodies stowed away in a pack that is solely their own.

Make this into a fun exercise and let your kids pick out a pack and then go over what is important to have in it.

So, for young kids (ages 5-12) ours contains the following items:

• Water bottle
• 4 Granola bars
• Hand-drawn map/directions to family/friends along with phone numbers (in case of separation)
• Fleece sweater, socks, t-shirt, & long-underwear
• Warm jacket
• Favorite "security blanket" item (this can be a small toy/doll/photo)
• Handheld video game or comic books
• Roll of quarters
• Flashlight
• Whistle

IS THIS WATER SAFE TO DRINK?

Water you can't live without it! Humans have gone 30+ days without food under survival conditions but you can't condition yourself to go without water regardless of your fitness level.

In a crisis, post-disaster waterborne diseases are going to be a major concern and diarrhea is a serious health issue that can imperil you and your family. Throughout the world, diarrhea is the number two infectious killer of children. The greatest danger comes from the accompanying dehydration, which is why having the right equipment for purifying water is critical.

If you have to use a questionable source in an urban environment, what should you do? There are three main ways of purifying water and they can be used for treating contaminated water in both urban and wilderness settings.

Mechanical
You can use a modern (hand pump) filter like an MSR or Sweetwater to treat water and remove any bacteria. These work best if you pre-filter the water through a bandanna or let the water sit in a pot for an hour to allow the debris to settle. I have used a variety of these over the years and some are better than others. Pick the brains of the local gear gurus at the outdoor store to see what's hot and then practice using it at home in your kitchen sink. I get many students who show up for a wilderness survival course with their filter still in the box and have no idea how (or if) it works!

Know the difference between a Water Filter and a Water Purifier. Water filters are the cheaper versions ($30+) and only remove micro-organisms like Giardia, which is what the average backpacker has to worry about. Water purifiers, on the other hand, remove both bacteria and viruses. Consider getting a purifier if you travel a lot to third world countries where hepatitis and meningitis are a concern. A quality Water Purifier will cost $100-$200, but is well worth it.

Survival Straws or Water Bottle Inserts have a very short life as they clog quickly and only last for a few liters of water. They are often sold as survival gear but spend a few extra pennies and get a decent water filter that will last for more than one drink.

One recent development is the Steri Pen. I have one and they are excellent for ultralight travel. The Steri Pen zaps the water with UV rays, essentially killing the bacteria and viruses. Insert the tip of the pen into a liter of clear water and turn on the switch for 60 seconds! You can find a Steri Pen for around $90 depending on online bargains. Batteries are required.

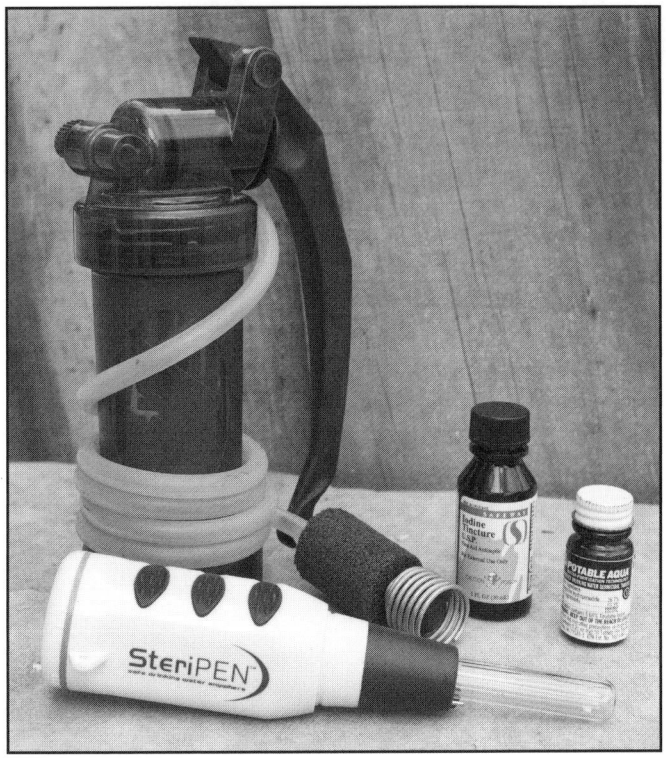

A mechanical MSR filter, SteriPen, and two examples of iodine for purifying water.

Chemical

Iodine is the most common chemical treatment method, though bleach can be used as well. The key with chemical treatment is to follow the manufacturer's directions. Many folks using iodine will add the tablets along with their Kool-aid/Crystal Light/Gatorade powder which will negate the iodine. You must wait the allotted 30 minutes (again check the label) before adding any powder or flavoring.

I like Potable Aqua brand which has 50 tablets per bottle and a shelf life of one year after it is opened. 2 tablets per quart of water is the recommended treatment. The only drawbacks: iodine is not good for pregnant women and those with thyroid problems. Again follow the directions.

Bleach (plain not lemon scented) can be used as well and is good for urban emergencies as most folks have a bottle in the laundry room. The usual amount is to add 8 drops of unscented bleach to 1 liter of water. Let it sit for 30 minutes before drinking.

Regarding long-term use, I have two friends, both of whom hiked the Appalachian Trail, and relied on either iodine or bleach as their sole water treatment method for up to 5 months without any ill effects. There are also chlorine dioxide tablets such as Aqua Mira which are similar to using bleach.

Try out a few different brands at home, see what the taste is like, and make sure there are no side effects before you rely on them in a crisis.

Boiling

Boiling kills viruses and bacteria but does nothing to remove chemical contaminants. Vigorously boil water for 1 minute. In an urban disaster, assume any water will be contaminated and purify it using any of the above methods. Boil it, filter it, or add the iodine but stay hydrated!

Don't Become Jerky

For about twelve years, I never used any type of water purification in the backcountry and regularly drank straight from lakes, springs, streams, water basins, and cow holes. I'd just drop down, drink, and grit my teeth to strain out the big stuff. I never had any problems. Speaking with my family doctor about this once, he said I probably had built up a resistance to things like Giardia. If you have the tools for treating water do so but, if not, don't die of dehydration.

Electrolyte Replacement Powders

Since I teach desert survival courses, some type of sodium supplement is necessary when working in the heat and is essential when pounding in a lot of water. Too much water in the body can result in hyponatremia which, if left untreated, can be life-threatening. Hyponatremia results when you are consuming copious amounts of water and diluting the sodium in your bloodstream. Technically you are hydrated (peeing clear fluid) but your electrolytes are whacked out.

If you live in a hot region, plan on carrying salty pretzels, chips, nuts or a few packets of sodium replacement powders like Hydralyte.

At home, you can make a simple rehydration drink using two common household items: In 1 liter of water, mix 1/2 a teaspoon of salt and 8 teaspoons of sugar. As nausea often accompanies dehydration and hyponatremia, drink small sips at first.

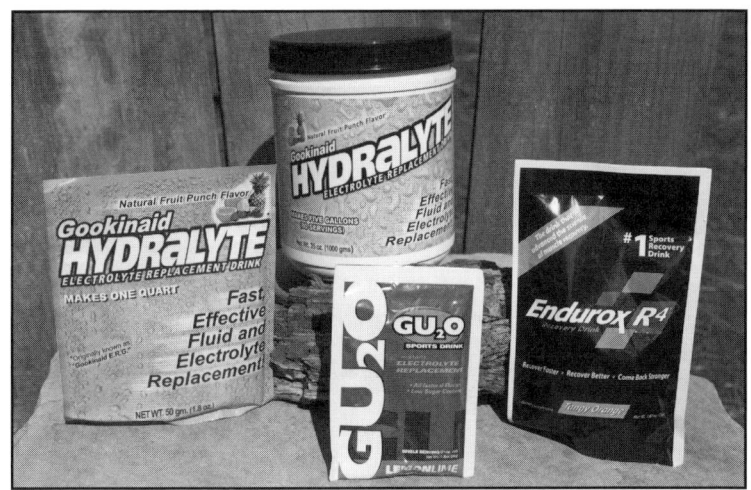

Sodium replacement powders for replenishing lost electrolytes.

FOOD FOR BEING ON THE MOVE

These food items differ from the type in your Home Kit where weight isn't an issue. They are lightweight, packed with nutrients, can be easily consumed (no cooking or little prep), and can be stowed nicely in the Shoulder Bag. I use many of these rations on our wilderness survival courses when covering a lot of mileage on foot.

Whatever grub you carry, keep in mind that you are striving for around 1200 calories a day minimum in your Shoulder Bag (more in a cold-weather environment where the body requires the calories and fat).

Myoplex, Met-RX, & Meal-Replacement Bars

Don't think lightweight granola bars. These are meal-replacement bars that bodybuilders use. They are packed with calories, high-protein (30-50 grams) and lots of vitamins and minerals. The Myoplex brand are preferred as they are the tastiest (like chocolate cake) and provide nutrients to last a few hours. There are also Met-Rx bars, PowerBar Hi-Protein, and Pure Protein bars. Try out a brand first before loading up your Shoulder Bag as some of these have a gag factor. You will need to consume plenty of water when taking in copious amount of protein like this.

Many students on my survival courses have noted that after two days of eating only these super concentrated bars, feelings of bloating and gastrointestinal discomfort, shall we say, start to surface. Remember this type of food is intended to carry you through a day or two while on the move. You will greedily welcome fresh fruit and vegetables after living on synthetic foods but they will do the job, providing necessary nutrients until your situation changes.

The best thing is that you can cram 6-8 of these in a small Shoulder Bag. With my high-metabolism, I usually need 4 bars a day (and lots of water) while hiking 15-20 miles a day cross-country. These meal-replacement bars are intended for adults not children.

SOS Rations

Sometimes called LifeBoat Rations, these vacuum-sealed food rations are compressed wheat, vegetable protein, sugar, and fat. They have a five-year shelf life and one pack contains 9 bars. Each bar contains 400 calories. Because they contain very little salt or topical oils, they don't make you thirsty. What I like about the SOS rations is they actually taste pretty good- much like shortbread. I usually consume 4 a day and prefer either these or the Myoplex route as far as modern "synthetic" food goes for ultralight travel.

MRE's

Meals Ready To Eat- what every soldier has had his fill of. They are high in calories and some are tasty but they take up too much space in the Shoulder Bag. You may want to strip these down to just the main entrée.

Clockwise from top: SOS survival rations, MRE, Salmon in a packet, Met-RX meal replacement bars.

Dehydrated Foods

These have come a long way in the past ten years. Mountain Home is one brand that I have used on the trail and they have fairly wholesome meals ranging from lasagna to Thai dishes. The only drawback is that they require hot water. Sample a few and see if you find them satisfying.

Jerky

Few foods for the pack fit the bill like jerky. This is homemade jerky or quality packaged jerky and not the processed stick jerky you find at every gas station checkout counter. Look in the health-food stores for the good stuff. I make my own jerky (only 24 hours hanging in the Arizona sun!) out of venison or store-bought strips of stir-fry beef. You can also use an electric food dehydrator.

Meal-Replacement Drinks

There are plenty of meal replacement drinks such as Muscle Milk, EAS Advantage, and Ensure that can are high in nutrients but I find these better suited for my vehicle kit than a Shoulder Bag as, not only are they too bulky, but I don't want to run the risk of them breaking open over my gear. These drinks are not for the lactose intolerant.

Vitamins

After a few days without sleep and proper nutrition your body is going to be suffering. It doesn't take up much space to pack in some multi-vitamins to supplement your diet so throw a dozen chewable vitamins in your kit. These can even be used to flavor iodine treated water. Vitamin C tablets, in particular, can be used to neutralize the iodine flavor.

EQUIPPING YOUR VEHICLE

You can have a great plan for evacuating and tons of great survival gear but if your vehicle isn't maintained properly, your exodus during a disaster could be short lived (and you too!).

Here are some things to factor in when equipping your vehicle:

-How far can you drive on a full tank of gas? Depending on the severity of the threat, the gas pumps may be quickly depleted by other evacuees so you may not be able to refill. I know that my passenger van loaded with people and gear will carry us 250 miles on one tank of fuel before needing a refill. This means that we could make it to a family member's place in the next state if necessary.

-How many passengers (pets included) can you reasonably fit in the vehicle along with your Home Bail-Out gear?

-Is it a manual (stick) transmission and can all the drivers in your family operate one?

-How much water do you have per person per day in the vehicle? This was a real shortcoming for many evacuees stuck on the freeway for hours in the searing heat during Hurricane Katrina. Drivers were literally trading gas for drinking water in some cases. The ideal amount is to have 2 gallons per person per day at the minimum.

Left to right: Air compressor, Gorilla power wrench, can of Fix-a-Flat, supply of water, and a quality jack.

Here's what I carry in my truck all year:

- Full size spare tire (get rid of the pretend tire the manufacturer provided)
- A spider jack
- Gorilla lug-wrench
- Mini air-compressor
- 2 cans of Fix-A-Flat Tire Repair
- 10 gallons of water
- Leatherman (or pliers & screwdrivers)
- Small folding shovel
- Roll of duct tape
- Headlamp
- Sleeping bag
- Wool hat
- Emergency blanket
- Insulated gloves
- Jar of peanut butter
- 4 Met-Rx Meal Replacement Bars
- Local and state maps
- Umbrella (instant shade and protection from the elements)
- Sunscreen
- Cell phone charger
- Satellite phone

An Ounce of Prevention

You know the saying and it applies to vehicle maintenance too. Taking a few minutes each month in your driveway to check the tire pressure along with the radiator, oil, and transmission fluid levels will be time well spent. Would you really want to add breaking down on the highway to your list of woes when fleeing an impending disaster?

Regarding tire changing gear, make sure you have a quality jack and lug wrench like the types listed. With the $20 air compressor and $5 can of Fix-A-Flat, you may not even have to be hunched over on the highway swapping out tires.

Rest In Peace

With the advances in outdoor gear in the last ten years, you can purchase a quality sleeping bag that compresses down to the size of a football. Get a bag rated to at least 32 degrees F for three-season use. For winter weather, get one rated to at least 0 degrees F.

When you purchase a bag, make sure you get one that has been hanging up in the store rather than stuffed in a sack for the past year. For home storage, keep it compressed in the sack only when you are on the move otherwise the fibers will get damaged and thus affect the insulating capabilities. When not in use, ours are hanging up next to the Home Kit.

COMMUNICATING AND REUNITING WITH FAMILY MEMBERS

How will you hook up with others in your family if great distance is involved? This is something you want to discuss NOW while life is calm. Do not plan on having cell phone coverage either. You may be in a remote area without cell towers or the lines may be overloaded from the disaster.

Unless you are particularly gifted at telepathic communication, I would suggest investing in two-way radios. These have become so affordable in recent years that it pays to have a charged set on hand. They are great for communicating between vehicles while on the road and some have ranges up to ten miles. Keep in mind that there is little privacy on the airwaves. Having a ham radio and/or CB would be even better but at least start with a set of two-way radios.

My wife and I also have an out of state family member whom we can contact in the event we become separated and need to relay messages to one another.

Sound In Orbit

Satellite phones have gotten more affordable over the last few years but keep in mind that they often have dead zones where you cannot get a signal for long periods of time. Once a signal is received, you may only have a few minutes to talk before losing reception so get out the critical details first (your location, medical needs, etc...) and then chat about the weather. SAT phones are not impact or water resistant so carry the phone in a padded, waterproof container along with a portable charger for the vehicle.

Strategies For Reuniting With Family Members

It's important to have a predetermined meeting spot where family members can hook up if they get separated during a hasty evacuation. Do you have a family member or trusted friend who can pick up your kids at school if you are stuck on the other side of the city? Where will you reunite with them?

Where great distance is involved, choose a city or destination in each of the four directions where you would head if evacuation were imminent. Not just the city but a specific location there, for example the Holiday Inn parking lot on Main Street on the east side of Portland.

I would also consider having your rendezvous location in a medium size town (say under 30,000 people) as there will hopefully be fewer problems with crime and gangs than in a large metropolis.

Have rendezvous information tucked in the vehicle glove box and in each child's Shoulder Bag along with relevant family phone numbers.

Left to right: Short Wave AM/FM radio, cell phone, and satellite phone for keeping in touch. During a disaster use text messaging which requires less band width than placing a call.

FINAL THOUGHTS

Just a few generations ago in this country, people knew how to build their own house, fix a car, repair plumbing, grow food in their garden, use medicinal plants for remedies, hunt, fish, skin a rabbit, stitch up their wounds, barter for goods with their neighbors, and sharpen an ax, to name a few skills.

My father, who was of the WWII generation, was one of those people and I am grateful to have gleaned insight into the seemingly forgotten world when we, as a society, were more self-reliant. I marvel at the ingenuity and skills of my forbearers who wrested a living from the land without whining about the weather or looking to someone else for a meal.

Our culture's mindset has changed considerably in just one generation though as it has shifted from self-reliance to a total dependency upon the "system." But what happens when the system fails, as it often does, when the bureaucracy of large government collides with the fury of a large-scale disaster? The prospect for survival falls back on the individual who now is left to fend for him or herself.

I think it's safe to assume that there will be future disasters and large-scale catastrophes so it pays to get in the habit now of providing for yourself and not depending on bureaucratic solutions. Beyond assembling some of the emergency kits listed in this book, here are five recommendations to help you prepare.

1. Sit down with your family, pull out a road atlas, and map out potential escape routes and rendezvous sites for each direction out of your city. Take into account what to do if your kids are at school or an elderly member needs evacuating. Discuss this family plan a few times a year to keep things fresh in everyone's head.

2. Take a basic First-Aid and CPR class. These are essential human skills that everyone should know. It is never time wasted and could save a life down the road. Then outfit your vehicle and emergency kits with a quality first-aid kit.

3. Gain some skills in self-protection especially if you are a single woman. This is like taking a First-Aid class. It is life insurance. Learn from an experienced instructor versed in practical self-defense or acquire skills in safely using a firearm.

4. Pay attention to what is happening in your community and the world at large with regards to disasters and terrorist attacks. Ask the "what if" questions for your region. If you work or live in a large city, determine what the exits are and the hazards associated with the building where you work.

5. Lastly, develop a flexible mindset and know deep down that if disaster strikes, you will not only survive but prevail. Becoming more self-reliant in your thinking and lifestyle will boost your confidence and put you on the path to safeguarding your family.

This book can only point out the strategies. It is up to you to take action now and do the rest. I wish you well on your journey towards greater independence and peace of mind.

Appendix 1:
Disaster Practice Scenarios

The following are some exercises that I have used in my survival classes to get the mental gears turning. I'm sure you can come up with specific disaster scenarios for your region.

Scenario 1

You are in the heart of the city driving home from work on the highway when you feel the rumbling of what will turn out to be a 8.0 earthquake sweeping over the region. After a short time, the damaged highway becomes impossible to navigate and those surface roads that are still passable are experiencing miles of gridlock.

It is late fall and there are three hours of sunlight left. You are 7 miles from home where your spouse and newborn son are anxiously awaiting your return. A stocked Shoulder Bag is in the trunk of your car along with plenty of water, a map, pistol, & ammo. Cell phones are clogged with activity.

What are your immediate priorities in the minutes that follow?

What is your plan of action while you still have daylight?

Is there anything you can salvage off the vehicle itself before you leave on foot that can help you?

What are your main concerns traveling on foot?

Scenario 2

You and your kids are leaving a football game a few minutes early. As you are getting in the car, you see an immense, gray cloud being carried by the wind over the stadium and notice the faint smell of what seems like pool chlorine in the air. The blair of emergency sirens resounds throughout the stadium as throngs of fans pile out into the parking lot.

Not wasting any more time, you floor it and drive over the curb on your hasty exodus from the parking lot enroute to the highway. As you speed away from the stadium, you catch glimpses of the billowing chemical cloud in your mirror and see people collapsing near the stadium.

With your immediate priority of escape met, you race towards home 20 miles away while hearing on the radio about a chemical spill on the railroad tracks. Cellphones are clogged and you can't get through to your spouse.

What is your plan of action?

If you leave the city, what is your escape route and where will you rendezvous with the rest of your family?

What about those family members who are unable (elderly, sick, etc…) to get out on their own? Will you be able to retrieve them?

Scenario 3

It is January and a winter storm is supposed to be rolling in late tonight. Your boss has you working overtime today and you won't get out of the office until 7 pm. At noon, you notice the weather is not minding the meteorologists as the first flurries come down with a vengeance. By 5 pm there is two feet of snow on the ground and you missed the news about a Winter Storm Warning. This means the storm is going to be a blizzard as a mass of polar air has swept into the region from the north causing the temperature to plummet.

You decide to leave but are already faced with 40 mph winds and a wind-chill of 20 below zero. The city has essentially shut down and services have come to a halt. The exposure to severe wind-chill can result in hypothermia and flesh can freeze in seconds. Reducing contact with the elements is critical.

The blinding snow has created drifts as you drive on to the interstate at a snail's pace. Keeping your truck on the road is a challenge despite your winter driving experience. After trudging along under white-knuckle conditions for an hour, you succeed in only getting eight miles down the interstate when you swerve to avoid another car and veer off the road into a deep snow bank. You are stuck!

After checking for injuries, you take a deep breath and run through your options. Fortunately you have a stocked Shoulder Bag, sleeping bag, winter boots, and extra food. The radio says the storm will linger for the next three days. Power is already out in many parts of the city and emergency services aren't likely to reach stranded motorists until the storm passes.

Your truck has a full tank of gas and provides shelter. Do you stay put or try to walk out? If you stay in the vehicle, run your engine fifteen minutes every hour and make sure to crack a window to avoid carbon monoxide poisoning.

What if someone else succumbs to your fate and gets stuck nearby, will you offer to share your precious rations and gear?

How will you obtain fresh water when your supply runs out? Do you have a container and know how to melt quantities of snow or ice?

What factors will affect your decision to leave?

Scenario 4

The much-dreaded bird flu has finally made the leap to humans and is now spreading throughout the globe in its first wave of virulence. No city, regardless of size or remoteness, can escape its wrath and the dead are beginning to pile up in your city. Health officials have urged people to stay home while public places like malls, libraries, and schools have closed. The power grid comes and goes with intermittent blackouts that last for days. The grocery stores empty out as hungry mobs overtake the weekly delivery trucks.

A black market for antibiotics, water, food, and other essentials has sprung up overnight and there are often groups of shady individuals hanging around your street. The police and National Guard, who were seen around the city early on in the pandemic, are now a rare sight as increasing numbers of gangs rule the night. According to officials, the pandemic and the lawlessness will only grow in intensity for another 12 months.

What are your daily priorities?

Who will be the designated individual who leaves the house to get food and medicine or take a sick family member to the hospital? What is the protocol for those staying behind in the house?

Will you allow the individuals leaving to re-enter or will they have their own quarantine area apart from the house and how will this affect safety and defense?

At what point, if any, do you decide to abandon your house and move elsewhere?

If the point comes where you have to leave the city, where will you go since other cities are similarly affected? Will you head to the hills, and if so, where is the nearest wilderness area and how well do you know it?

Appendix 2:
Pocket Emergency Contact Card

Make copies of these, cut them out, and give to everyone in your family.

Emergency Contact Card for Kids

Mom's Cell Phone:_____

Dad's Cell Phone: _____

Out of State Family: _____

Meeting place if separated: _____

Emergency Contact Card for Kids

Mom's Cell Phone:_____

Dad's Cell Phone: _____

Out of State Family: _____

Meeting place if separated: _____

Appendix 3:
Survival Gear, Training Courses
and Resources

Ancient Pathways
The author's Arizona-based company provides comprehensive survival training courses for individuals and groups throughout North America. Programs range from 1-21 days up to 9 weeks. Ancient Pathways also carries survival kits, books, Mora knives, and emergency-related gear. Visit www.apathways.com or call 928-526-2552.

Equipped To Survive
Colleague Doug Ritter's voluminous survival website contains a wealth of gear reviews as well as insightful commentary on previous disasters. Visit www.equipped.org for more information.

Hoods Woods Video Series
Veteran survival instructor Ron Hood's videos cover everything from making survival kits to trapping and urban survival skills. Visit www.survival.com for more information.

Chris Nyerges School of Self-Reliance
Great courses and books on preparedness, foraging, food procurement, and urban survival. Visit www.christophernyerges.com or call Chris in Los Angeles at 1-626-791-3217.

Wilderness Medicine Institute
Intensive courses on wilderness medicine ranging from 2-30 days in length as well a good selection of first-aid kits. Visit www.nols.edu/wmi or call 1-866-831-9001.

Suarez International
Gabe Suarez offers some of the finest training courses in self-protection and firearms instruction anywhere. Visit www.suarezinternational.com or call 928-776-4492.

Paxton Quigley
Her books on self-protection and firearms training for women are outstanding. She teaches seminars throughout the U.S. Visit www.paxton-quigley.com for information.

AWARE
Self-protection seminars for women covering skills that really work on the street. Visit www.aware.org or call 1-877-672-9273.

Emergency & Disaster-Related Websites

How To Prepare For Disasters, University Of Illinois
http://web.extension.uiuc.edu/disaster/prep.html

State Offices and Agencies of Emergency Management
http://www.fema.gov/about/contact/statedr.shtm

Emergency Preparedness Checklist By State
http://www.ready.gov

American Academy of Pediatrics- Disaster Preparedness Information For Families and Young Children
http://www.aap.org

Resources: Where To Purchase Quality Gear

Sportsman's Guide
Outdoor and survival gear company offering discounted military surplus, ponchos, tents, sleeping bags, and a fine array of clothing. Visit www.sportsmansguide.com or call 1-800-888-3006.

Adventure Medical Kits (AMK)
AMK has set a new standard for comprehensive first-aid kits for either individual or group use. Visit www.campmor.com or call 1-800-226-7667.

Lehmans
Tons of non-electric products for those seeking greater self-sufficiency and independence. Visit www.lehmans or call 1-888-438-5346.

Nitro-Pak
Supplier of survival kits, dehydrated food, and disaster-related gear. Visit www.nitro-pak.com or call 1-800-866-4876.

REI
Small line of survival products along with an extensive array of clothing and footwear. Visit www.rei.com or call 1-800-426-4840.

Wiggy's Sleeping Bags
Fine selection of outdoor clothing, gear, and the best sleeping bags in the business. Visit www.wiggys.com or call 1-866-411-6465.

Bibliography

CNN Reports: *Katrina- State of Emergency*, Andrews McMeel Publishing, 2005.

Burns, August A. *Where Women Have No Doctor, A Health Guide For Women*, The Hesperian Foundation, 1997.

Forgey, William. *Wilderness Medicine: Beyond Basic First-Aid*, Globe Pequot Pr., 1999 (5th ed.).

Lewellyn, Harry. *Shifting Into 4WD, The SUV Owner's 4WD Handbook*, Gem Guides, 2002.

McDevitt, Ian. *Tactical Medicine*, Paladin Press, 2001.

Nester, Tony. *Desert Survival Tips, Tricks, & Skills*, Diamond Creek Press, 2003.

Nester, Tony. *Practical Survival Tips, Tricks & Skills*, Diamond Creek Press, 2001.

Quigley, Paxton. *Not An Easy Target, Self-Protection For Women*, Fireside Publisher, 1995.

Redlener, Irwin. *Americans At Risk: Why We Are Not Prepared For Megadisasters And What We Can Do Now*, Alfred A. Knopf Publishers, 2006.

Stark, Peter. *Last Breath: Cautionary Tales From the Limits of Human Endurance*, Ballantine Books, 2001.

Suarez, Gabe. *The Combative Perspective: The Thinking Man's Guide To Self-Defense*, Paladin Press, 2003.

Werner, David. *Where There Is No Doctor, A Village Health Care Handbook*, The Hesperian Foundation, 1992.

*If you liked this book, then check out our other titles
in the series by Tony Nester:*

Practical Survival Tips, Tricks, & Skills

The first book in the series covers how to prepare for emergencies in a forested environment. Topics and skills include: anatomy of survival situations and how to avoid them, lostproofing skills, critical gear every hiker should carry, how to start a fire in wet weather, water purification methods, field-expedient shelters, signal mirror use, and more. Filled with detailed photos and practical tips.

$10.95 plus $3 shipping.
Available at www.apathways.com or Amazon.com.

Desert Survival Tips, Tricks, & Skills

The second book in the series focuses on the skills and strategies for adapting to arid regions. Topics covered include: survival psychology, clothing selection, heat-related injuries and how to avoid them, shade shelters, the latest treatment methods for venomous bites and stings, water location tips, myths regarding water consumption in the desert, preparing kids for desert trips, and how to equip your vehicle. Jammed with photos and pragmatic skills.

$10.95 plus $3 shipping.
Available at www.apathways.com or Amazon.com.

About the Author

Tony Nester has been teaching bushcraft and survival courses since 1989. His company Ancient Pathways provides survival training courses for the U.S. Military, National Park Service, the Grand Canyon Field Institute, and corporations throughout the Southwest. Tony has been featured on NBC News, the Discovery Channel and in Outside Magazine. He resides in Flagstaff, Arizona with his family.

For information on survival field courses, corporate training seminars, or lectures, contact:

Ancient Pathways, LLC
www.apathways.com
928-526-2552